■ SCHOLASTIC
# News
## Nonfiction Readers

# Pluto

## by
## Christine Taylor-Butler

SCHOLASTIC INC.

New York  Toronto  London  Auckland  Sydney
Mexico City  New Delhi  Hong Kong  Buenos Aires

These content vocabulary word builders
are for grades 1-2.

Consultants: Daniel D. Kelson, Ph.D.
Carnegie Observatories
Pasadena, CA
and
Andrew Fraknoi
Astronomy Department, Foothill College

Curriculum Specialist: Linda Bullock

Photo Credits:

Photographs © 2005: Lowell Observatory: 5 bottom right, 11; NASA: cover, 5 top right; Photo Researchers, NY: 2, 5 top left, 15 (Chris Butler), 1, 4 bottom right, 7, 23 right (Lynette Cook), back cover, 4 top, 13, 19 (Lynette Cook/SPL), 4 bottom left, 5 bottom left, 9 (Detlev van Ravenswaay); PhotoDisc/Getty Images via SODA: 23 left.

Book Design: Simonsays Design!

ISBN 0-516-25081-7

12 11 10 9 8 7 6 5 4 3 2        5 6 7 8 9 10/0

Printed in the U.S.A.                08

First Scholastic paperback printing, October 2005

# CONTENTS

# WORD HUNT

Look for these words as you read. They will be in **bold**.

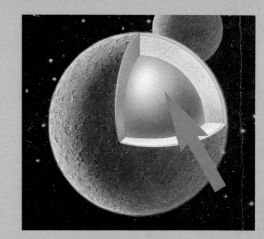

**core**
(kor)

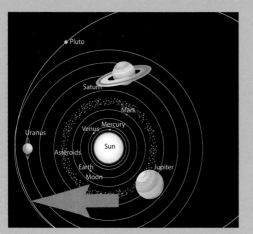

**orbit**
(**or**-bit)

**Pluto**
(**ploo**-toh)

4

**moon**
(moon)

**Neptune**
(**nep**-toon)

**solar system**
(**soh**-lur **siss**-tuhm)

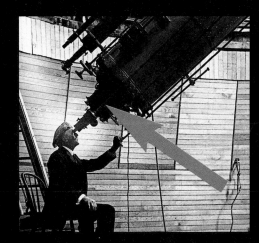

**telescope**
(**tel**-uh-skope)

# Pluto!

Pluto is very far away.

No picture has ever been taken of the surface of Pluto.

All the pictures of Pluto are painted by artists.

**An artist drew this picture of Pluto.**

Pluto is the ninth planet from the Sun.

It is made of rock and ice and has its own **moon**.

Pluto is the smallest planet in the **solar system**.

**Pluto**

**Sun**

9

Pluto is hard to see.

It is hard to see even with a giant space **telescope**.

No spaceship has ever visited Pluto.

Percival Lowell was an astronomer. He searched for Pluto for many years but did not find it.

Scientists know that Pluto is made of both rock and ice.

The outside of Pluto is mostly solid ice.

The inside is called the **core**.

Scientists are not sure how much of the core is rock or ice.

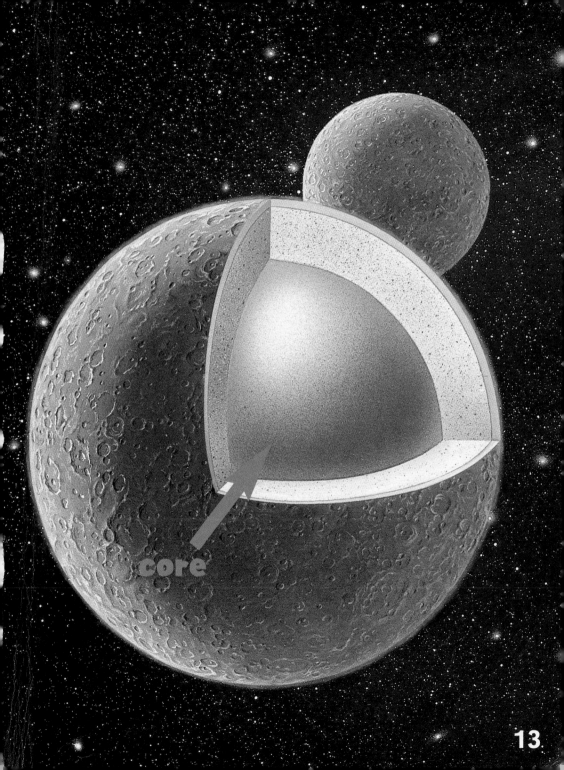

core

Pluto has its own moon.

It is called Charon.

Charon and Pluto look alike. They both look like icy balls, but Charon is smaller than Pluto.

Pluto

Charon

Charon is about half the size of Pluto.

Pluto goes around the Sun on a path called an **orbit**.

The path of most planets is shaped like a circle.

Pluto's path is shaped like an oval.

Sometimes Pluto's orbit crosses **Neptune's** orbit.

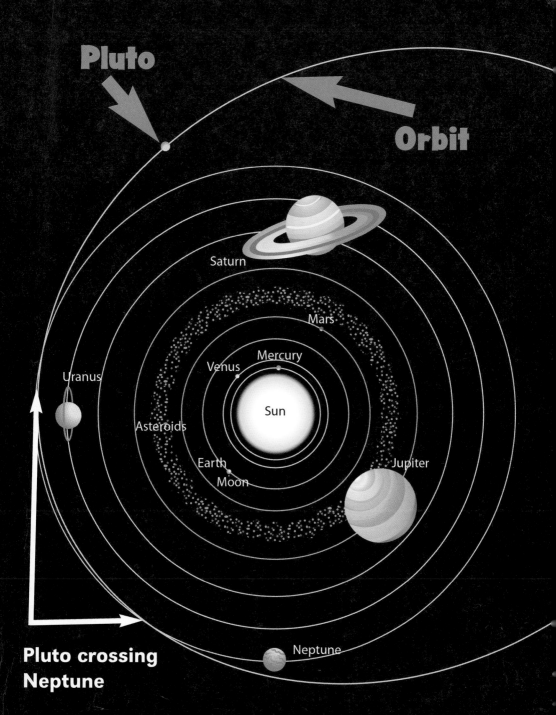

Pluto

Orbit

Saturn

Mars

Mercury

Venus

Uranus

Sun

Asteroids

Earth

Moon

Jupiter

Neptune

**Pluto crossing
Neptune**

In 2226 Pluto will cross Neptune's orbit.

But Pluto will still be far away.

From the surface of Pluto, the Sun will still look as small as a star.

Will we know what Pluto really looks like by 2226?

Maybe!

Sun

Pluto

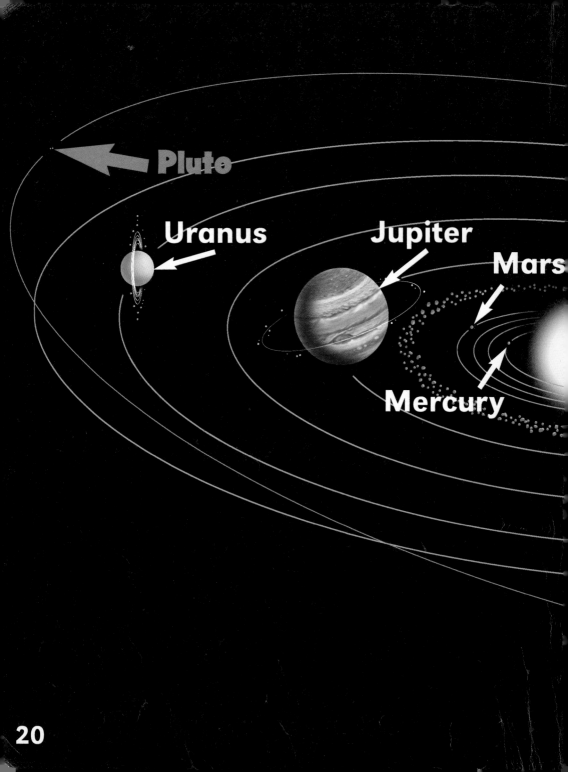

Pluto

Uranus

Jupiter

Mars

Mercury

# IN OUR SOLAR SYSTEM

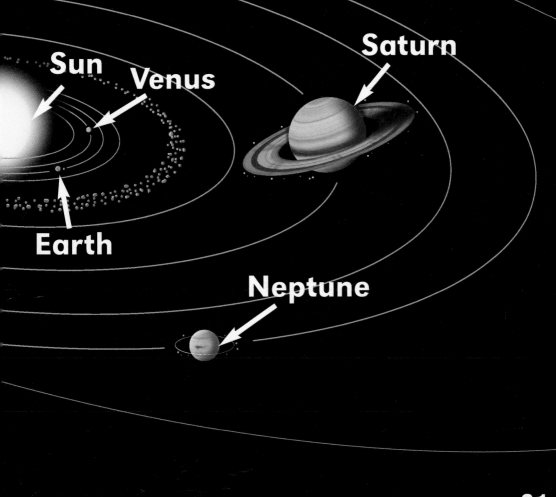

Sun

Venus

Saturn

Earth

Neptune

# YOUR NEW WORDS

**core** (kor) the inside of a planet

**moon** (moon) an object that
    circles a planet

**Neptune** (**nep**-toon) a planet named for
    the Roman god of the sea

**orbit** (**or**-bit) a path around an object

**Pluto** (**ploo**-toh) a planet named for the
    Roman god of the underworld

**solar system** (**soh**-lur **siss**-tuhm) the
    group of planets, moons, and other
    things that travel around the Sun

**telescope** (**tel**-uh-skope) a tool used to
    look at things in space

# Earth and Pluto

A year is how long it takes a planet to go around the Sun.

 **Earth's year**
**=365  Earth days**

**Pluto's year**
**=90,553 Earth days**

A day is how long it takes a planet to turn one time.

 **Earth's day**
**= 24 hours**

**Pluto's day**
**= 153 Earth hours**

A moon is an object that circles a planet.

 **Earth has**
**1 moon**

**Pluto has**
**1 moon**

Did you know that a spacecraft called *New Horizons* will leave for Pluto in 2006? But it will take 10 years to fly there!

# INDEX

## FIND OUT MORE

**Book:**
*Children's Atlas of the Universe,*
By Robert Burnham
Reader's Digest Children's Publishing, Inc., 2000

**Website:**
Solar System Exploration
http://sse.jpl.nasa.gov/planets

## MEET THE AUTHOR:

**Christine Taylor-Butler** is the author of more than 20 books for children. She holds a degree in Engineering from M.I.T. She lives in Kansas City with her family, where they have a telescope for searching the skies.